LETTERS TO MBA STUDENTS

WISDOM. CLARITY. CAREER. LIFE.

DR. ASHISH GUPTA

To every student who ever sat in class wondering,
"Is this really for me?"

To the ones who dared to ask deeper questions,
who stayed back after lectures,
who failed, tried again, and chose growth over comfort.

And to the mentors, teachers, and guides
who show up every day —
not just to teach business,
but to build humans.

This book is for you.

With gratitude and belief,
Ashish Gupta

Contents

Contents

Copyright

Preface

Every year, thousands of students enter B-schools with dreams in their eyes and questions in their minds.

They're told to build their résumé, crack placements, master frameworks, and become industry-ready.
But no one tells them how to deal with self-doubt, how to lead themselves first, how to think clearly, or how to navigate rejection with grace.
No one tells them that the MBA is not just a degree — it's a mirror, a playground, a pressure-cooker, and most importantly, a launchpad for life.

Over the past 14+ years, I've had the privilege of working closely with students across India — in classrooms, counseling rooms, corridors, and career bootcamps.
And in all these interactions, I saw a gap:
Not in ambition — but in awareness.
Not in talent — but in direction.
Not in potential — but in perspective.

That's why this book exists.

Letters to MBA Students is not a textbook.
It's a collection of 30 heartfelt letters — short, powerful, and personal — written as if I were sitting across the table from you.

These letters are about real things:

- How to find your purpose

- How to choose the right specialization
- How to handle rejections and pressure
- How to network, present, communicate, and lead
- How to grow through your MBA, not just go through it

Each letter is a reflection of the conversations I've had with students just like you — sometimes after a tough day, sometimes before a life-changing decision, and often, in moments of quiet transformation.

You don't have to read them all at once.
Read one a day. Or one a week. Or one when you need a nudge.
And more than reading them — feel them.
Pause. Reflect. Apply.

Because the MBA isn't the end goal.
It's the beginning of your journey toward becoming not just a better professional — but a better human.

If even one letter in this book makes you stop, think, and realign — then this work has served its purpose.

Let's begin.

With purpose,
Ashish

Prologue

Dear MBA Student,

Before you read the first letter, I want you to pause.

Take a breath.
Forget the deadlines, the grades, the placement pressures for just a moment.
And ask yourself:
"Why did I choose this path?"

Not the fancy version for interviews.
The real one — the one that lives inside your heart.

Because that's what this book is really about.

It's not about cracking exams — it's about cracking your own code.
It's not about topping the class — it's about understanding yourself.
It's not about chasing job titles — it's about building a meaningful life.

In the rush of B-school, we often forget to pause, reflect, and realign.
We start focusing more on speed than on direction.

That's where these letters come in.

Each letter in this book is written like I would write to a student I deeply care about —

One who's talented, ambitious, full of potential, but sometimes confused, tired, or overwhelmed.
One who doesn't need another lecture, but a **conversation.**
One who needs a voice to remind them — you're not alone.

These letters will not give you formulas.
They'll offer you something more powerful:
Clarity. Confidence. Calm.

So read them slowly.
Let them speak to the part of you that often stays silent —
the part that's quietly asking:
"Am I on the right path?"

You are.
You're just figuring it out. And that's okay.

Let these letters walk with you — from confusion to clarity, from pressure to purpose, from MBA... to MBL: **Master of Building Life.**

Let's begin the journey, together.

With all my heart,
Ashish

Introduction: Why This Book Matters

Dear Future Leader,

In a world full of competition, information overload, and endless hustle, doing an MBA today means a lot more than just attending classes, acing exams, and landing a job. It's about shaping who you are and who you're going to become.

MBA isn't just a degree. It's a journey of transformation.

Yet, what most students don't realize is that the real transformation doesn't just happen in classrooms or through textbooks — it happens in conversations, in reflections, and in moments of uncertainty, growth, and self-discovery.

That's where this book comes in.

"Letters to MBA Students" isn't a textbook. It's a companion.

A mentor in the form of words. A guiding light through the fog of confusion. A reminder that you are not alone on this journey.

Over the last 14 years of working with some of the top universities and interacting with thousands of students, I've seen the difference between those who merely survive their MBA and those who truly thrive. It's not always about grades or IQ. It's about **clarity, character, consistency,** and the ability to make the right decisions at the right time.

These letters are born from real conversations, real struggles, and real experiences. Whether it's finding your purpose, building the right skillset, learning how to lead, or simply dealing with rejection or burnout — this book offers you one letter at a time, one lesson at a time.

This book matters because **you matter.**

You are the future entrepreneur, executive, changemaker, or leader who will shape not just companies but communities, ideas, and the nation's future. And for that, you need more than just an MBA – you need wisdom, mindset, and direction.

So read these letters when you're confused, when you're stuck, or when you simply need a spark. Come back to them as often as needed. Let them speak to you in moments when you need clarity, courage, or just a gentle nudge to keep going.

Because the world doesn't need more degree holders.

It needs more self-aware, ethical, bold, and visionary leaders.

And that's exactly who you are becoming.

Welcome to the journey.

With purpose and belief,
Ashish

About The Author

Dr. Ashish Gupta is a passionate educator, mentor, and strategic leader with over 14 years of experience in higher education, specializing in Admissions, Outreach, and Student Success. As the Director of Admissions & Outreach at RV University, Ashish has guided thousands of students toward building meaningful careers and purposeful lives.

Beyond administrative excellence, Ashish is deeply committed to human potential — especially in India's youth. His writing, public speaking, and mentorship are focused on personal growth, leadership, clarity, and conscious decision-making. His career guidance models and training programs have impacted students across India, especially in Tier 2 and Tier 3 cities.

Ashish is on a mission to create one million future-ready students and believes that education must go beyond degrees — it must empower individuals to build a fulfilling life.

"Letters to MBA Students" is not just a book — it's an extension of Ashish's daily work, conversations, and care for the next generation of leaders.

You can connect with Ashish on:
LinkedIn: https://www.linkedin.com/in/theashishgupta/
Website: www.ashishgupta.co.in
Email: authorashishgupta@gmail.com

Part 1: The Inner Foundation

CHAPTER I

Discover Your Why Before You Chase the How

Dear MBA Student,

You've made it to an MBA program. That alone speaks volumes about your capabilities, drive, and potential. But let me ask you something that very few will:

Why are you here?

Not how you got in. Not what you plan to do. But why?

Why did you choose to do an MBA?
Why does this journey matter to you?
Why do you want success, and what does that success truly look like?

You see, most students get busy chasing the how —
"How do I get an internship?"
"How do I crack placements?"
"How do I build my resume?"
"How do I get a high-paying job?"

But very few pause to ask —
"Why do I want what I want?"

And yet, that's the question that shapes everything.

Your why is your anchor.
Your why is your compass.
Your why is the fuel that keeps you moving when things get tough — and they will.

If your why is just "money" or "status," you'll find yourself burnt out or lost sooner than you think. But if your why is rooted in **purpose** — to build something, to solve real problems, to uplift others, or to become the best version of yourself — you'll find joy even in the struggle.

The most successful people I've met in the corporate world, startups, or public service didn't just know what they were doing — they had absolute clarity on why they were doing it.

And here's the truth: Once your why is clear, the how becomes easier. You attract the right people, the right opportunities, and make better decisions.

So today, I invite you to pause.

Grab a notebook. Sit with yourself. And write down:

- Why did I choose to pursue an MBA?
- What kind of life and impact do I want to create?
- What would make this journey truly meaningful for me?

There are no right or wrong answers. Only honest ones.

MBA is not just a course. It's a reset button. A second chance to choose consciously.

So don't waste it chasing someone else's idea of success.

Find your why. Own it. Live it.
And let it guide you through every decision you make here.

With clarity comes confidence.
And with confidence, comes unstoppable momentum.

Rooting for you,
Ashish

CHAPTER II

Be Curious, Not Just Ambitious

Dear MBA Student,

Ambition is celebrated — and rightly so.
We love people who aim high, chase big goals, and want to make something of themselves.

But here's a little secret I've learned after years of working with students, professionals, and leaders:

Ambition without curiosity is like a car with no fuel.

It may look sleek. It may sound impressive. But it won't go very far.

In the MBA world, you'll find ambition everywhere —
People chasing the best internships, fighting for top placement packages, gunning for leadership roles, building startups.

But how many are truly curious?

Curious about how businesses work,
Curious about human behavior and what drives decisions,
Curious about how ideas become revolutions,
Curious about their own strengths and blind spots.

The best MBA students I've seen aren't just ambitious — they're hungry to learn.

They ask questions.
They explore beyond the syllabus.
They talk to people outside their comfort zone.
They read not to impress but to understand.

Curiosity turns lectures into life lessons.
It turns group projects into insights about teamwork and leadership.
It turns campus interactions into lifelong networks.
It turns a summer internship into a career breakthrough.

Ambition says, "I want to reach the top."
Curiosity asks, "What can I learn from every step of the journey?"

And here's the irony — curious people often go further than the merely ambitious. Because while ambition can tire you out, **curiosity keeps you energized**. It makes learning fun. It keeps you open, adaptable, and innovative — traits every leader needs.

So don't just chase titles or salaries.
Chase knowledge. Chase understanding. Chase growth.

In every course, every conversation, every challenge — ask yourself:
What can I learn from this?

If you stay curious, you'll not only become successful — you'll become wise.

And that, my friend, is far more powerful.

Stay curious, stay humble, stay unstoppable.

With warmth and belief,
Ashish

CHAPTER III

Learn to Lead Yourself First

Dear MBA Student,

You've come here to learn leadership — to eventually lead teams, companies, movements, or maybe even nations.

But here's something most management books and MBA classrooms often miss:

You cannot lead others until you learn to lead yourself.

Self-leadership is the foundation of every form of leadership.
Without it, titles are hollow, and influence is temporary.

So, what does it mean to lead yourself?

It means showing up — even when no one is watching.
It means setting goals and following through — not for applause, but because you said you would.
It means taking responsibility for your actions, your mindset, your growth — every single day.

The greatest leaders I've met have mastered the ability to manage themselves:

- Their time
- Their energy
- Their emotions

- Their focus
- Their habits

They don't wait for motivation. They create discipline.
They don't blame circumstances. They take ownership.
They don't let fear stop them. They keep moving forward.

In an MBA program, you'll be taught how to lead teams, run businesses, and make strategic decisions. But remember — none of that will matter if your personal life is chaotic, your habits are weak, and your mindset is reactive.

Self-leadership is waking up early to work on your craft.
It's reading beyond what's required.
It's being honest with yourself about where you're slacking and where you're shining.
It's saying no to distractions and yes to growth.

Start with yourself.
Because when you learn to lead your own thoughts, habits, and emotions — people will naturally start trusting you to lead them too.

You don't need a title to be a leader.
Start today — lead yourself.

With deep faith in your potential,
Ashish

CHAPTER IV

Build a Growth Mindset – Every Day

Dear MBA Student,

You've heard it before — growth mindset is the key to success.
But here's the part most people miss:

It's not a one-time shift. It's a daily practice.

A growth mindset isn't just believing you can improve — it's choosing to improve, every single day.

In your MBA journey, you'll face competition, rejections, tough feedback, maybe even failure. Some students shrink in those moments. They take it personally. They lose confidence.
But those with a growth mindset? They see those same moments as lessons, not losses.

Here's the difference:

Fixed mindset says: "I'm not good at finance."
Growth mindset says: "I can learn finance if I stay consistent."

Fixed mindset says: "I'm bad at public speaking."
Growth mindset says: "I can become better by practicing regularly."

Fixed mindset says: "Others are smarter."
Growth mindset says: "I'll focus on becoming 1% better every day."

The truth is — you're not here to prove yourself.
You're here to improve yourself.

Every case study you read, every group project you do, every rejection you face — is a part of your growth if you let it be.

Here's how you build a growth mindset daily:

- Replace self-doubt with self-talk: "I'm learning."
- Embrace feedback, even when it stings — it's a mirror, not an attack.
- Reflect on progress, not just outcomes.
- Surround yourself with people who push you to grow.
- Celebrate effort, not just results.

Your MBA is not just preparing you for your first job — it's preparing you for every challenge life throws at you after that.
So grow your mindset like a muscle.
Train it. Test it. Stretch it. Strengthen it.

Because the person who grows daily will always outpace the person who settles early.

Your mindset is your magic. **Protect it. Practice it. Power it.**

On your side, Ashish

CHAPTER V

Confidence Comes from Competence

Dear MBA Student,

Let's talk about confidence.

Everyone wants it. Many fake it. Some wait for it to magically appear. But few truly understand where it comes from.

Here's the truth I want you to remember:

Real confidence doesn't come from talking big — it comes from knowing your stuff.
Confidence comes from competence.

You don't become confident by standing in front of a mirror saying, "I'm amazing."
You become confident when you do the work, build your skills, and show up prepared — again and again.

Think of any confident speaker, leader, or entrepreneur you admire.
They didn't start off that way.
They earned their confidence — through hours of practice, countless failures, constant improvement, and a relentless commitment to learning.

In your MBA life, you'll face moments that test your confidence:

- A tough classroom discussion
- A surprise interview question
- A presentation in front of industry leaders
- Competing with smarter peers

In those moments, remember:
You don't need to be the loudest in the room. You need to be the most prepared.

Confidence is quiet. It doesn't boast. It shows.
It shows in your depth of knowledge.
It shows in your calm under pressure.
It shows in how you respond, not react.

So instead of asking, "How can I become more confident?", ask:
"How can I become more competent?"

Read more. Practice more. Ask more questions. Seek feedback. Go deeper.
And with every new skill mastered, every gap filled, every challenge overcome — your confidence will rise naturally.

The best part? No one can take that confidence away from you.
Because you didn't borrow it — you built it.

Build your competence, brick by brick.
And soon, you'll walk into any room knowing — you belong there.

Keep building, Ashish

CHAPTER VI

Embrace Discipline, Not Just Motivation

Dear MBA Student,

Motivation is exciting, isn't it?

You watch an inspiring video, hear a powerful speech, or read a success story — and suddenly, you feel unstoppable. You tell yourself, "I'm going to change everything starting now."

But then... a few days pass. That spark fades. Distractions return. And you're back to old habits.

Here's a truth you'll learn sooner or later:

Motivation is temporary. Discipline is dependable. Motivation can get you started, **but only discipline keeps you going.**

If you want to succeed in your MBA journey — and beyond — you need to build systems, not just wait for sparks.

Discipline is:

- Showing up for class even when you're tired
- Finishing that assignment even when no one is pushing you

- Reading that extra case study when your friends are binge-watching
- Waking up early not because you feel like it but because you promised yourself you would

Discipline isn't about being perfect. It's about being consistent.
And that's what separates the top 5% from the rest — not talent, not luck, but relentless consistency.

You won't always be motivated.
Some days will be hard. Some nights will be long.
But if you've trained yourself to do the work anyway, you'll still grow.

That's the secret of high performers — they don't rely on moods.
They rely on habits.

So don't chase motivation. Build discipline.
Create routines that protect your goals.
Commit to small wins every day.
And trust that your efforts, even on the dullest days, are compounding into something powerful.

Success isn't one big motivational burst.
It's a quiet, daily commitment to keep moving forward — even when no one's watching.

Choose discipline. It will never fail you.

With discipline and belief, Ashish

Part 2: Career Clarity & Planning

CHAPTER VII

Don't Just Do an MBA – Build a Career Vision

Dear MBA Student,

It's easy to get caught in the whirlwind of MBA life — classes, case studies, assignments, internships, placements, and endless deadlines.
But pause for a moment and ask yourself this:

Are you just doing an MBA, or are you building a career vision?

There's a difference — a big one.

Doing an MBA without a vision is like driving a high-speed car without a destination. You'll go fast, but where are you actually going?

Many students enter business school thinking the MBA itself is the goal. But the degree is only a tool — a means to an end. Your real goal should be clarity about the life and career you want to build.

So here's a truth I want you to hold close:

An MBA will open doors — but you must know which door to walk through.

That's where your career vision comes in.

Ask yourself:

- What kind of work excites me?
- What problems do I want to solve?
- What values do I want my career to reflect?
- What kind of impact do I want to create?
- Do I want to build, lead, innovate, manage, teach, or serve?

The more clarity you build during your MBA, the less you'll drift after it.

Having a vision doesn't mean you need to know the exact job title or company you'll work for. It simply means you know your direction.
And when you know your direction, every choice — every internship, elective, project, mentor — becomes more intentional.

Don't follow the crowd.
Don't chase what's popular.
Chase what aligns with your strengths, your values, and your long-term dreams.

A job lasts a few years.
A career shapes your life.

So don't just build a resume — build a roadmap.
Don't just prepare for Day Zero — prepare for decades to come.

Your MBA is a golden opportunity to design the life you want.
Use it well.

With vision and purpose,
Ashish

CHAPTER VIII

How to Choose the Right Specialization

Dear MBA Student,

One of the most important decisions you'll make during your MBA journey is choosing your specialization. Marketing, Finance, HR, Business Analytics, Operations, Strategy, or even Entrepreneurship — the options are many, and so is the confusion.

Here's the advice I want to give you straight:

Don't choose a specialization based on trends. Choose it based on your strengths, interests, and long-term career vision.

Too many students pick specializations based on:

- What their seniors chose
- What's currently paying well
- What sounds "cool" or prestigious
- What others expect them to do

But here's the truth:

The wrong specialization can lead you into the right company but the wrong role — and years of regret.

So how do you choose the right specialization?

1. Know Yourself First

Start by understanding your interests, personality, and working style.

- Do you enjoy numbers and analysis? Finance or Business Analytics may fit.
- Do you love creativity and consumer behavior? Marketing could be your space.
- Are you a people person who enjoys building teams? HR might be perfect.
- Are you fascinated by supply chains and operations? Look into Ops or Strategy.

2. Reflect on Past Experiences
    What subjects did you enjoy during undergrad?
What internships or projects did you love (or hate)?
What kind of work energizes you?

Past behavior is often a clue to future satisfaction.

3. Explore Before You Decide

Attend all classes with an open mind in your first term.
Talk to professors, seniors, and alumni from each domain.
Intern or shadow someone in a field you're considering.

4. Think Long-Term, Not Just First Job

Will this specialization still excite you 5-10 years down the line?
Does it open doors in areas you're passionate about?
Don't just think about "what pays more today."
Think about "what gives you joy, growth, and value tomorrow."

5. Mix Passion with Practicality

You don't need to choose between passion and practicality. Find that sweet spot — what you're good at, what you enjoy, and what the market values.

Remember: **It's not the specialization that makes you successful. It's how deeply you master it, apply it, and grow within it.**

Choose wisely.
Because when you love what you do, work becomes a playground — not a prison.

Rooting for your clarity,
Ashish

CHAPTER IX

Make Internships Your Playground for Growth

Dear MBA Student,

When students hear the word "internship," most immediately think of one goal — PPO (Pre-Placement Offer).

That's great if it happens. But let me tell you something even more important:

Your internship is not just a job trial. It's a growth lab — a playground where you discover what kind of professional you want to become.

Internships are your chance to:

- Test your skills in the real world
- Understand how businesses actually operate
- Observe leaders and learn from them
- Try, fail, learn, improve — and repeat
- Reflect on what excites you and what doesn't

You're not expected to be perfect during your internship. But you are expected to be curious, proactive, and committed to growth.

Here's how to make the most of your internship:

1. Enter with a Learning Mindset, Not Just a PPO Mindset: Don't act like you're just there to impress. Be there to absorb, engage, and evolve. People remember learners more than show-offs.

2. Ask More Questions Than You Answer: Don't pretend to know everything. Ask "why" and "how" more often. Let your curiosity drive your learning.

3. Go Beyond the Job Description: Once you complete your assigned tasks, look for areas where you can add value. Be the intern who contributes, not just one who completes.

4. Build Relationships, Not Just a Resume: Internships are an amazing opportunity to build your professional network. Connect with mentors, teammates, and even fellow interns. These relationships can shape your career for years to come.

5. Document Your Learnings: Keep a daily or weekly log of what you're learning — about the industry, the work culture, the tools, and yourself. It'll help you during final placements and interviews too.

6. Seek Feedback and Act on It: Don't wait till the end. Ask for feedback midway. Learn what you can improve and actually do it. That shows maturity and coachability — traits employers love.

An internship is a rare window where you're allowed to make mistakes and ask basic questions without being judged — use it!

This is your practice ground before the real match begins. Make every day count.

Because you're not just interning to get a job —
You're interning to build a career, develop clarity, and become future-ready.

Play well. Learn fast. Grow deep.

In your corner always,
Ashish

CHAPTER X

Jobs vs Careers – Think Long-Term

Dear MBA Student,

As you move through your MBA journey, you'll hear a word over and over again — placements.
Everyone talks about the "job" — the package, the company, the role, the Day 0 dream.

And while yes, your first job matters — I want to remind you of something far more important:

A job is a step. A career is the journey. Don't confuse the two.

The biggest mistake young professionals make is chasing jobs, not building careers.

A job gives you a salary.
A career gives you satisfaction.
A job may impress others.
A career must fulfill you.
A job can be taken away.
But a career is something you build, skill by skill, decision by decision.

Let me ask you:

- Are you choosing a role because it's truly aligned with your strengths and vision?

- Or are you choosing it just because it sounds impressive on LinkedIn?
- Are you thinking about what will look good in one year?
- Or what will help you grow over ten?

Here's how to think long-term:

1. Don't Chase Titles — Chase Skills

What you learn in the early years will shape your ability to lead, innovate, and grow later. Choose roles that teach, stretch, and challenge you.

2. Ask: Where Will This Take Me in 5 Years?

Will this job help you move closer to your vision? Does it open doors to things you care about? Or is it a detour that looks glamorous but leads nowhere?

3. Prioritize Growth Over Comfort

The best career decisions often feel uncomfortable in the beginning — new city, new industry, steep learning curve. But they build resilience and experience.

4. Stay True to Your Inner Compass

Don't compare your path with others. What's right for your friend may not be right for you. The long game is about alignment, not applause.

MBA gives you options. Lots of them. But clarity will help

you choose wisely.

- **Build a career you won't need a vacation from.**
- Build a career that excites you on Monday mornings.
- Build a career that evolves as you evolve.

A job starts your journey. But your career — that's your legacy.

Make decisions your future self will thank you for.

Thinking long-term with you,
Ashish

CHAPTER XI

Build Your Career Capital – One Skill at a Time

Dear MBA Student,

You've probably heard this phrase often: "Build your career."
But what does that really mean?

Does it mean chasing high-paying jobs?
Or collecting certifications and titles?
Or simply moving up the corporate ladder?

Here's how I want you to think about it:

Every successful career is built on a foundation of skills — not just degrees.
And those skills become your **career capital.**

Career capital is the value you carry with you wherever you go — the strengths, abilities, and experiences that make you useful, respected, and in demand.

While job titles can change and companies can fold, your career capital is yours forever.
And the best part? You don't build it overnight. You build it one skill at a time.

Here's how you can start:

1. Identify High-Value Skills in Your Chosen Domain

If you're into marketing, can you analyze campaigns and write compelling copy?
In finance, can you interpret data and explain it clearly to non-finance folks?
In operations, can you manage teams and implement processes?

Stacking complementary skills gives you an edge that others can't easily replicate.

2. Go Deep, Then Go Wide

Master one core skill deeply — become really good at it.
Then gradually build around it. This makes you both specialized and versatile.

3. Practice > Theory

You don't become great at Excel by reading about Excel.
You become great by using it daily — in projects, internships, side hustles.
Turn knowledge into skill through action.

4. Leverage Every Opportunity to Learn

Each class, project, presentation, competition, or internship is a training ground.
Approach it like a craftsman — always refining your tools.

5. Document and Reflect

Maintain a simple "Skills Journal." After every major task or assignment, ask yourself:

- What skill did I use?
- What did I learn?
- What can I improve?

That's how awareness turns into mastery.

Don't wait for your dream job to build your skills. Build your skills so your dream job finds you.

The most successful professionals aren't necessarily the most talented — they're the most skilled.
They've invested in themselves, consistently and patiently.

So instead of asking, "How do I get ahead?", start asking:
"What can I learn today that my future self will thank me for?"

Build your career capital.
Because when you're rich in skills, opportunities will chase you.

One skill at a time,
Ashish

CHAPTER XII

Learn to Network Like a Pro (Without Being Salesy)

Dear MBA Student,

When people hear the word networking, they often picture awkward small talk, fake smiles, and forced conversations. But that's not real networking. That's transactional behavior.

True networking is not about **collecting contacts — it's about building connections.**

The most powerful networks are built on authenticity, value, and trust — not desperation, flattery, or business cards.

As an MBA student, your network can become one of your greatest assets. But to make it meaningful, you need to change your mindset from "What can I get?" to "How can I connect?"

Here's how to network like a pro — without feeling salesy or fake:

1. Start with Genuine Curiosity

People love talking about themselves — their work, experiences, struggles, and success.

Ask thoughtful questions. Listen deeply.
Be genuinely interested — not just in what they do, but why they do it.

2. Give Before You Ask

Share an article, give feedback, offer help, or even just express appreciation for someone's work.
Small acts of value go a long way in building trust.

3. Quality > Quantity

You don't need a massive LinkedIn network. You need meaningful relationships.
Focus on 10 real connections, not 100 random ones.

4. Follow Up, Don't Fade Away

After meeting someone, send a thank-you note or message.
Keep in touch — share your updates, congratulate them on milestones, or occasionally check in.
Networking is nurturing.

5. Be Yourself, Not a Salesperson

People sense authenticity. Don't pretend to be someone you're not.
You don't need to pitch yourself constantly — your energy, work ethic, and curiosity will speak louder.

6. Leverage Campus Interactions

Your classmates, professors, guest speakers, alumni —

they're all part of your potential network.
Treat every interaction with respect and intentionality.
Some of your strongest professional connections will begin with a simple classroom conversation.

7. Play the Long Game

You don't build a network for today's benefit. You build it for life.
Some connections will help you after a year, some after a decade. That's the beauty of it.

Networking isn't about climbing ladders — it's about building bridges.

And here's the final truth:
The best time to build your network is when you don't need anything.
That's when connections feel real, not transactional.

So show up with sincerity, stay curious, be generous — and watch how doors open, not just for jobs, but for mentorship, collaboration, and life-changing opportunities.

Your future network is waiting — start today, the right way.

In connection and support,
Ashish

Part 3: Skill Building for the Real World

CHAPTER XIII

Learn Communication – It Will Open Doors

Dear MBA Student,

You might have chosen Marketing, Finance, HR, or Business Analytics as your specialization — but let me tell you something that cuts across every field, industry, and leadership role:

Communication is the one skill that will open more doors for you than any other.

In the MBA world, people often obsess over technical skills, industry trends, and strategic models. And yes, those are important.
But your ability to **express ideas clearly, listen actively, and influence people positively** — that's what will set you apart.

Think about it:

- A great idea means nothing if you can't pitch it well.
- A job interview is just a conversation where clarity meets confidence.
- A team fails when there's misunderstanding, not just mismanagement.
- Even a data analyst who can tell a story with numbers will shine brighter than one who can't.

Communication is not about speaking more — it's about connecting better.

Here's how to sharpen your communication muscle:

1. Master the Art of Listening

Great communicators don't just speak well — they listen deeply.
When you listen, you understand. When you understand, you respond wisely.

2. Think Before You Speak or Write

Ask yourself:

- What's the purpose of what I'm saying?
- Who is my audience?
- What tone will create the right impact?

Good communication is not about saying more — it's about saying the right thing at the right time, in the right way.

3. Write with Clarity, Speak with Impact

Whether it's an email, report, LinkedIn post, or boardroom presentation — your ability to structure your message matters. Learn storytelling, formatting, and brevity.

4. Practice Public Speaking, Even If It Scares You

Join a Toastmasters club. Take part in class presentations.
Record yourself speaking and watch it back.
The only way to get better is to do it — again and again.

5. Work on Your Body Language

Your tone, posture, eye contact, and facial expressions communicate just as much — if not more — than your words.

6. Feedback is Your Best Friend

Ask your peers and mentors:

- Was I clear?
- Did I engage you?
- How can I improve?

Then act on that feedback. That's how growth happens.

In a world full of noise, those who communicate with clarity, empathy, and confidence will always stand out.

It's not about being the loudest voice in the room — it's about being the clearest, the kindest, and the most compelling.

So whatever your career dreams are — start investing in communication today. It's not just a soft skill.
It's a power skill.

Speak well. Write well. Connect well.

And the world will listen.

Communicating with you,
Ashish

CHAPTER XIV

Presentation is a Power Skill

Dear MBA Student,

Let me say it upfront — if there's one skill that can instantly raise your visibility, boost your confidence, and make you stand out in a room full of equally talented people, it's this:

Presentation is not just a skill — it's a power skill.

In your MBA journey, you'll be presenting all the time — case studies, group projects, pitches, ideas, research, business plans. But most students treat presentations as assignments.
Smart students treat them as opportunities — to influence, lead, and be remembered.

Whether you're pitching an idea to a professor or proposing a solution to a real company problem, your presentation isn't just about slides — it's about storytelling, structure, and self-confidence.

Here's how to master this power skill:

1. Start with the Story, Not the Slides

Before you touch PowerPoint, ask:

- What's the core message?
- What's the problem and what's the proposed solution?

- Why should the audience care?

Your job is not to inform, but to inspire and influence.

2. Structure is Everything

Every strong presentation has a simple flow:
Hook → Problem → Insight → Solution → Impact → Call to Action
Clarity wins over complexity — always.

3. Design Matters (But Keep It Simple)

Avoid clutter. Use visuals, graphs, icons, and whitespace wisely.
One message per slide. Keep text minimal. Your slide supports you — it shouldn't speak for you.

4. Your Delivery is the Deal Maker

Voice modulation. Eye contact. Confident body language. Practice your tone, pace, pauses, and energy. The way you say it matters as much as what you say.

5. Practice, Practice, Practice

Rehearse like a pro. Record yourself. Time yourself. Get feedback.
Every great presenter you admire is not "naturally gifted" — they're well-practiced.

6. Connect with Your Audience

Make it interactive. Ask questions. Tell relevant stories. Use examples that matter to them.
Presentation is not a monologue — it's a conversation with impact.

7. End with a Bang, Not a Whimper

Don't just trail off with "That's it."
End with a strong closing line, a memorable insight, or a bold call to action.

In a world full of data, the one who can present it clearly becomes the leader.

MBA students with strong presentation skills get noticed in class, picked for team leads, appreciated in internships, and remembered by recruiters.

So don't just complete your next presentation. Own it.
Because every time you present, you're not just showing slides —
You're showcasing who you are.

Present boldly,
Ashish

CHAPTER XV

Master the Art of Problem Solving

Dear MBA Student,

You've chosen to pursue a degree that teaches you to lead, manage, strategize, and build.
But here's a skill that lies at the heart of everything you'll do — in class, in your career, and in life:

The ability to solve problems. Clearly. Calmly. Creatively.

Every business exists because it solves a problem.
Every job role, every project, every team — they all revolve around one thing:
How well can you solve challenges?

Companies don't hire you just for your degree.
They hire you for your thinking — your ability to assess a situation, break it down, and offer meaningful solutions.

So if there's one skill you must commit to mastering during your MBA, it's this:
The art of problem solving.

Here's how to develop it:

1. Fall in Love with the Problem, Not the Solution

Don't rush to answer. First, understand the problem deeply.
Ask:

- What's really going on here?
- What are the root causes?
- Are we treating symptoms or solving the source?

Clarity begins with questions.

2. Break it Down

Every big problem can be divided into smaller, manageable pieces.
Use frameworks like:

- SWOT (Strengths, Weaknesses, Opportunities, Threats)
- 5 Whys
- First Principles Thinking
- MECE (Mutually Exclusive, Collectively Exhaustive)

The structure clears the fog.

3. Think from Multiple Angles

The best solutions come when you see the problem from multiple perspectives — customer, company, competitor, and culture.
What's obvious to one side might be invisible to another.

4. Use Data, But Don't Ignore Intuition

Back your ideas with evidence. Numbers bring credibility.
But never underestimate your own common sense, empathy, and real-world observation.

5. Practice Through Case Studies

Your MBA classroom is a live lab. Every case study is a mini battlefield.
Go beyond just finding the "correct answer."
Instead, focus on how you approach the issue, why you choose a solution, and what assumptions you're making.

6. Communicate Your Solution with Clarity

It's not enough to have a solution.
You must be able to explain it clearly — to your team, your professor, your client, or your CEO.
That's where structured thinking and storytelling matter.

Problem solvers are leaders. They stay calm under pressure, bring clarity to chaos, and take action when others freeze.

And here's the best part — this skill never expires.
Whether you're in consulting, marketing, HR, finance, or entrepreneurship — your ability to solve problems is your superpower.

So train your mind. Tackle real-life challenges. Build that muscle.
Because every challenge you solve now... prepares you for something bigger tomorrow.

Solving alongside you,
Ashish

CHAPTER XVI

Data is Gold – Learn to Use It

Dear MBA Student,

There's a new currency in today's world. It's not just money, degrees, or even connections.
It's **data.**

In today's business landscape, data is gold — but only for those who know how to use it.

As an MBA student, you're training to become a decision-maker. But here's the thing — good decisions are rarely based on guesswork anymore. They're based on insights drawn from data.

Whether you're in marketing, finance, HR, operations, or strategy — your ability to understand, interpret, and act on data will define your success.

So, let's make one thing clear:

You don't need to become a data scientist. But you must become data-smart.

Here's how to start:

1. Get Comfortable with Numbers

Don't run away from charts, dashboards, or spreadsheets.

Embrace them.
Learn how to read trends, patterns, and anomalies.
Numbers don't lie — they tell powerful stories.

2. Learn the Basics of Tools

Excel is non-negotiable.
Also explore tools like Power BI, Tableau, or Google Data Studio — even at a basic level. You don't have to master them, but you should know how to ask the right questions and make sense of what you see.

3. Turn Data into Insights

Raw data means nothing until you ask:

- What is this data telling me?
- What decisions can I make with this?
- What's the action plan?

Decision-makers aren't looking for reports. They want insights — and that's what you must learn to deliver.

4. Use Data in Your Presentations

Want to impress in class, interviews, or real-world meetings?
Back up your ideas with numbers. A well-placed statistic or data visualization can elevate your pitch instantly.

5. Understand the Ethics of Data

With great power comes great responsibility.
Don't manipulate data to fit your story. Let integrity guide how you collect, interpret, and present facts.

6. Blend Data with Empathy

Never forget — behind every number is a human story.
The best professionals know how to balance data with intuition, logic with emotion, numbers with narratives.

In the digital age, the professionals who win are those who can translate data into direction.

So don't fear data. Don't avoid it.
Learn it. Use it. Master it.

Because in a world full of noise, data gives you clarity.
And clarity leads to great decisions — the kind leaders are made of.

Digging for gold with you,
Ashish

CHAPTER XVII

Build a Personal Brand While You Learn

Dear MBA Student,

Let me ask you a simple question:
When someone says your name, what comes to their mind?

That, right there, is your personal brand.
And whether you realize it or not — you already have one.

Your personal brand is not about logos, taglines, or social media followers.
It's about your reputation, your value, and what you're known for.

In a world where everyone is chasing credentials, the ones who stand out are those who have crafted a clear identity — and communicated it with consistency.

So here's my message to you:
Don't wait to build your brand after your MBA. Start while you learn.

Why Does Personal Branding Matter?

- It helps you get noticed in a crowded job market.

- It positions you as a go-to person in your area of interest.
- It attracts opportunities — internships, interviews, collaborations, even clients.
- And most importantly, it gives you clarity about what you stand for.

How to Build Your Brand (Without Bragging)

1. Find Your Focus

What are you passionate about? What's your core strength? What do you want to be known for — marketing insights? Startup strategy? Finance analysis? Public speaking?
Clarity is the first step to branding.

2. Show Up Online — Authentically

Create a strong, clean LinkedIn profile. Start sharing what you're learning — insights from a case study, your internship experience, lessons from a book, or reflections from a guest lecture.
Be real. Be valuable. Be consistent.

3. Add Value, Not Noise

Your brand grows every time you help someone, share useful content, or start meaningful conversations — both online and offline.
Remember: it's not about you — it's about what you bring to others.

4. Be the Same Person Everywhere

Whether in class, on stage, in meetings, or online — let your actions match your message.
Consistency builds trust. Trust builds your brand.

5. Create Before You Graduate

Write blogs, record videos, host podcasts, or run campus events. Create content that reflects your interests and your journey. One well-crafted post can open unexpected doors.

Your degree gives you credibility. But your brand gives you visibility.
And in today's world, visibility is opportunity.

So don't just learn passively. Build actively.
Let people know who you are, what you care about, and where you're headed.

Because the world doesn't just reward talent —
It rewards those who know how to position that talent.

Start now. Build as you go.
Your future self will thank you.

Shaping brands and futures with you,
Ashish

CHAPTER XVIII

Collaboration Over Competition

Dear MBA Student,

In an environment full of ambitious people, tight deadlines, and high-stakes placements, it's easy to fall into the trap of thinking:

"I have to beat others to succeed."

But here's a powerful shift I want you to make — one that will change not just your MBA journey, but your entire career:

Choose collaboration over competition. Every time.

Yes, the corporate world is competitive. But it also thrives on teamwork, trust, and synergy. The most successful people aren't lone wolves — they're team players who lift others as they rise.

Let's be honest — competition can push you to do more. But too much of it can:

- Create anxiety
- Breed jealousy
- Damage relationships
- Make you feel isolated

Collaboration, on the other hand, builds:

- Deeper understanding
- Better outcomes
- Stronger networks
- Lifelong friendships

During your MBA, you'll work in group projects, case competitions, internships, and club activities. These aren't just tasks — they're training grounds for the real world.

Here's how to embrace collaboration like a leader:

1. Shift from "Me" to "We"

Ask not just "How can I win?" but "How can we win together?"
Your leadership is defined by how well you bring people together, not how far you run alone.

2. Recognize Others' Strengths

Everyone brings something to the table — analytical thinking, creativity, presentation skills, empathy. Spot those strengths. Celebrate them. Leverage them.

3. Share, Don't Hoard

Share resources, notes, referrals, insights.
Helping others doesn't reduce your chances — it multiplies your goodwill.

And remember: what goes around, comes around.

4. Give Credit Generously

If someone contributed to your success, acknowledge them publicly.
Great collaborators give credit. Great competitors crave it.

5. Network with Abundance, Not Insecurity

Your classmates aren't your enemies — they're your future co-founders, teammates, mentors, and champions. Build relationships, not rivalries.

Real growth happens when smart people work with each other, not against each other.

You're not here to outshine your peers. You're here to grow with them.

Because after all, life isn't a race — it's a relay.
And the ones who learn to pass the baton, share the victory.

Choose collaboration. Build bridges. Create win-wins.

Together is always better.

In unity and strength,
Ashish

Part 4: Navigating Campus Life

CHAPTER XIX

Choose Growth Over Comfort

Dear MBA Student,

Every day during your MBA, you'll be faced with choices.

Some will be easy — familiar, safe, comfortable.
Others will stretch you — challenging, uncertain, even scary.

And here's the truth you need to remember:
Growth and comfort don't coexist.
If you truly want to grow, you must learn to get comfortable being uncomfortable.

- Most students play it safe:
- Picking the easy elective
- Avoiding public speaking
- Sticking to known circles
- Choosing internships that feel secure but don't excite them
- Staying away from risks that might lead to failure (and learning)

But here's what the top 1% of MBA students do differently —

They lean into discomfort.

They:

- Join clubs even if they're shy
- Volunteer to lead group projects, even if they're not the best speaker
- Take the harder course because they know it'll sharpen their skills
- Say yes to that internship in a new city, new industry, or new domain

Why?

Because they understand one thing:

Comfort is cozy, but it rarely leads to transformation.

Growth, on the other hand, might be awkward and uncomfortable in the moment — but it elevates you for life.

Here's how you can start choosing growth every day:

1. Do One Hard Thing Every Week

Speak up in class. Pitch an idea. Ask a professor a tough question. Attend a networking event alone. Get used to feeling stretched — it's a sign you're evolving.

2. Embrace Failure as Feedback

If you're not failing at anything, you're probably not challenging yourself enough.
Failures don't define you. They refine you.

3. Ask for Constructive Criticism

Don't settle for "You did great." Ask:

- "What could I have done better?"
- "Where did I lose the audience?"
- "What skill do I need to improve?"

Feedback stings before it strengthens.

4. Surround Yourself with Growth-Minded People

Hang out with peers who push you to aim higher, think deeper, and step up. Comfort zones shrink when you're in the company of doers.

5. Keep a Growth Journal

Every time you take a risk, write down what you learned — not just the outcome. You'll start to see patterns of how far you've come.

MBA is not a destination. It's a launchpad.
And no rocket ever launched from a comfort zone.

So say yes to the challenge. Choose the tougher path when it aligns with your purpose. Trust that the discomfort you feel now is the tuition you pay for greatness.

Push yourself. Surprise yourself.
Grow, every single day.

Cheering for your discomfort-fueled growth, Ashish

CHAPTER XX

How to Make the Most of Your MBA Campus

Dear MBA Student,

Walk around your campus for a moment — look at the lecture halls, the café corners, the library, the amphitheatre, the faculty offices, and the endless conversations happening around you.

Now pause and realize this:

Your MBA campus is not just a place to study. It's a mini-world where you build your network, shape your identity, and discover your potential.

You'll only be here for 18 to 24 months. But the choices you make on this campus will echo for years to come — in your career, relationships, and confidence.

So don't just attend classes.
Immerse. Engage. Make it count.

Here's how to truly make the most of your MBA campus life:

1. Be Present, Not Just Enrolled

Show up — not just physically, but mentally and

emotionally.
Attend events. Join discussions. Participate in workshops.
Great things don't happen in isolation — they happen when
you show up consistently.

2. Build Real Connections

Your classmates aren't just batchmates — they're your
future co-founders, collaborators, mentors, and friends for
life.
Go beyond small talk. Learn their stories. Add value. Lift
each other up.

3. Use Every Resource Available

Your campus has mentors, guest lectures, clubs, labs,
incubators, and networking opportunities. Most students
underuse them.
The successful ones squeeze every drop out of what's
available.

4. Get Involved Beyond Academics

Join student clubs. Lead initiatives. Organize events.
Represent your college.
Leadership isn't a course — it's a practice. And your
campus is your training ground.

5. Form a Circle That Pushes You to Grow

Find people who challenge your thinking, share big ideas,
and support your goals. The right peer circle can accelerate
your learning more than any textbook.

6. Be Curious, Be Everywhere

Attend sessions from other domains. Interact with alumni.
Explore cross-functional areas.
You never know which small exposure might shape your
big decision.

7. Build a Campus Legacy

Do something that adds value to the ecosystem — a project,
a podcast, a research paper, a new initiative.
Let your time here be remembered for something
meaningful.

**MBA is not just a degree. It's an ecosystem. A playground.
A mirror. A launchpad.**

And your campus is at the center of it all.

So don't just pass through it. Live it. Breathe it. Own it.
Because when the final term ends and you look back — it
shouldn't just be a blur of lectures and deadlines.

It should be a collage of experiences, friendships, moments,
and growth.

Make every corner count.

Exploring with you,
Ashish

CHAPTER XXI

Learn From Your Peers – Everyone Has a Story

Dear MBA Student,

When you look around your classroom, what do you see?

Future consultants, marketers, analysts, founders?
Group members? Competitors? Friends?

Here's what I want you to really see:
A goldmine of experiences, perspectives, and stories — sitting right next to you.

In an MBA program, you're not just learning from professors, books, or industry guests.
You're learning from your peers — and that might just be one of the richest learning opportunities you'll ever have.

Every person you meet on campus brings with them a story:

- A failed startup
- A turnaround at their last job
- A personal struggle that shaped their grit
- A perspective shaped by their hometown, culture, or industry
- A unique way of thinking or solving problems

And the best part? You have unfiltered access to these stories — in coffee breaks, hostel rooms, group discussions, club meetings, late-night debates, and everyday conversations.

But most students miss it. Why?

Because they only interact with peers for what's required — assignments, projects, parties.
They never listen deeply, ask real questions, or go beyond the surface.

Don't make that mistake.

Here's how to truly learn from your peers:

1. Practice Deep Listening

Ask about their journey. What shaped them? What failures did they grow from? What motivates them? Be curious, not transactional.

2. Respect Different Backgrounds

Your peers may come from different cities, languages, industries, and belief systems. Their lens may be different from yours — and that's where learning happens.

3. Collaborate Across Strengths

Notice who's great at finance, storytelling, leadership, or negotiation. Learn from their strengths, and share yours.

You grow when you exchange, not just compete.

4. Have Meaningful Conversations

Go beyond gossip and grades. Talk about aspirations, failures, worldviews, big ideas. Real conversations build real connections.

5. Reflect on What You Learn

After every group project, club meeting, or debate, ask yourself:

- What did I learn from others?
- What surprised me?
- What can I apply in my own life?

Everyone has a story. But not everyone takes the time to listen.

If you learn to do that now — truly listen, observe, absorb, you'll walk away from your MBA with more than a degree. You'll walk away with wisdom, empathy, relationships, and perspective.

So before you aim to impress the world, learn from the world that's right next to you — your peers.

Because one day, you'll realize...
They were some of your best teachers.

In conversation and curiosity, Ashish

CHAPTER XXII

Stay Away from the Toxic Trio – Gossip, Ego & Negativity

Dear MBA Student,

Your MBA journey is filled with opportunities to learn, lead, and grow. But just like any high-energy environment, it also has its traps.

And there are three traps in particular that can silently kill your potential — I call them the Toxic Trio:

Gossip. Ego. Negativity.

They don't appear in your curriculum. But if you don't learn to avoid them, they'll silently eat away at your focus, your relationships, and your growth.

Let's break them down:

1. Gossip: The Shortcut to Nowhere

It may feel entertaining. It may make you feel included. But gossip is a low-vibration activity that creates more harm than fun.

Talking about people never builds your character.
Talking to people, with honesty and kindness, does.

Avoid the urge to engage in drama. Don't contribute to whispers and backdoor opinions.

Instead, build a reputation for being trustworthy and positive. People remember that far longer than your clever jokes.

2. Ego: The Enemy of Growth

You're smart. You've made it to a good program. But let me remind you:

Ego says, "I already know."
Growth says, "I'm here to learn."

Ego makes you defensive, competitive, and closed off. It stops you from asking questions, taking feedback, or admitting mistakes.

The best leaders are not those who know everything — they're the ones who are always willing to learn from everything.

So drop the need to always be right. Choose humility. It's a superpower in disguise.

3. Negativity: The Silent Poison

MBA life can be stressful — deadlines, competition, uncertainty. But if you surround yourself with people who constantly complain, blame, and spread pessimism, it will affect your mindset and energy.

Protect your environment. Be the person who sees

possibilities, not just problems.
Yes, express concerns — but with solutions. Stay grounded — but also stay optimistic.

Positivity isn't blind hope. It's a choice to move forward with strength, no matter the situation.

Here's the Golden Rule:

Be the kind of person others trust, admire, and feel better after speaking to.

And that happens when you:

- Speak with kindness
- Learn with humility
- Lead with optimism

Stay away from the toxic trio — because your time, energy, and attention are too valuable to waste on things that don't help you grow.

You didn't come this far to fall for small distractions.
You came here to rise.

Stay focused. Stay clean. Stay powerful.

With strength and clarity,
Ashish

CHAPTER XXIII

Use Failures as Feedback, Not Labels

Dear MBA Student,

Let's talk about something that no one enjoys but everyone experiences — failure.

You might mess up a group project.
You might not get shortlisted for that dream internship.
You might freeze during a presentation.
You might face rejection even after giving your best.

And in those moments, a small but dangerous thought might whisper in your mind:

"Maybe I'm not good enough."

But here's what I want you to remember — and truly believe:

Failure is not a label. It's just feedback.

It doesn't say, "You're a loser."
It simply says, "Here's what you can learn. Here's how you can grow."

The problem is not that we fail. The problem is that we take failure personally. We wear it like a tag on our identity.
But successful people don't do that.
They look at failure like a mirror — not a judgment.

Here's how to turn failure into fuel:

1. Feel it, But Don't Dwell in it

It's okay to be disappointed. Sit with it. Process it. But don't stay stuck in self-pity.
Ask: "What can I do next?" instead of "Why did this happen to me?"

2. Extract the Lesson

- Every failure has a message.
- Was it lack of preparation?
- A communication gap?
- A mismatch of expectations?

Write it down. Reflect. That's your goldmine.

3. Take Ownership, Not Blame

Blaming others or making excuses weakens you. Owning your part empowers you.
Say, "Here's what I could have done differently." That's maturity.

4. Seek Feedback from the Right People

Ask mentors, professors, or peers: "What could I improve?" Don't just ask for praise. Ask for growth guidance.

5. Try Again — Smarter, Stronger

Resilience isn't about never falling. It's about bouncing back better every time.

MBA is not just about learning business. It's about learning how to bounce back.

You'll fail in small ways and big ways — and that's okay. Because every setback is setting you up for a stronger comeback.

Let go of the fear of failing. Hold on to the power of learning.

You're not a failure just because something didn't work out. You're a work-in-progress, and every experience is shaping the masterpiece you're becoming.

So next time you stumble, smile and say —
"This is feedback, not a verdict."

And keep moving forward.

Rooting for your growth, always,
Ashish

CHAPTER XXIV

Be Active, Be Visible, Be Valuable

Dear MBA Student,

There's one simple truth about life on campus — and in the real world:

If people don't see you, they can't value you. And if you're not valuable, being seen won't matter.

You need all three:
Be Active – take initiative
Be Visible – show up consistently
Be Valuable – contribute meaningfully

Let's break it down.

1. Be Active – Show Initiative

Don't just be a passive participant in your MBA journey.
Raise your hand in class. Lead a student club. Volunteer for events.
Start something — a study circle, a podcast, a campus newsletter.

You'll never grow sitting on the sidelines.

Opportunities are given to those who show up before being asked.

2. Be Visible – Let People Know You Exist

You might be talented. You might have great ideas.
But if no one knows you, how can they recommend you?
Support you? Collaborate with you?

Visibility doesn't mean self-promotion. It means presence.

- Ask questions in sessions
- Share insights on LinkedIn
- Talk to professors after class
- Introduce yourself to guest speakers
- Attend networking events

You don't have to be loud. Just be consistent, curious, and visible where it matters.

3. Be Valuable – Always Add Value

Don't just show up. Contribute.
Be the teammate who delivers on time. Be the one who shares resources. Be the person others want to work with.

Ask yourself regularly:

"Am I adding value in this class, this project, this conversation, this group?"

Value could be in the form of ideas, effort, energy, or empathy. You don't have to be the smartest — just be helpful and reliable.

Why does this trifecta matter?

Because when you're active, people notice.
When you're visible, opportunities find you.
When you're valuable, people remember you.

Your MBA campus is a mini version of the world. And in both, those who participate with purpose rise faster than those who just quietly "get by."

Don't wait for placements to prove your worth. Start now. Build your presence, one meaningful action at a time.

Be the student people admire, trust, and recommend — not just because you showed up, but because you made a difference.

Active. Visible. Valuable.

Every single day.

Cheering you on,
Ashish

Part 5: Preparing for the Future

CHAPTER XXV

Be Future Ready – Learn, Unlearn, Relearn

Dear MBA Student,

The world you're preparing for is not static. It's not even slow. It's rapidly changing, constantly evolving, and brutally unpredictable.

New technologies. Shifting industries. Emerging roles. Changing customer behavior.
What's relevant today might be outdated tomorrow.

So, how do you stay future-proof in a world that refuses to stand still?

By mastering the most important skill of all: the ability to Learn, Unlearn, and Relearn.

Let's break that down:

1. Learn – Stay Curious, Stay Updated

MBA is not the end of your learning. It's the beginning of learning how to learn.
Read beyond your syllabus. Follow trends in your industry. Experiment with new tools.
Treat learning like your daily habit, not just an exam strategy.

In the age of AI and automation, the curious will always have an edge.

2. Unlearn – Let Go of Old Patterns

This is the hardest part.
Sometimes, what got you here won't take you there.

You may need to:

- Unlearn outdated frameworks
- Unlearn biased assumptions
- Unlearn habits that no longer serve your growth

Being willing to say, "Maybe I was wrong," is not weakness — it's wisdom.

3. Relearn – Adapt & Rebuild with Fresh Eyes

What you thought you knew might need a new perspective. Relearn how to communicate in a digital-first world. Relearn leadership in a hybrid workspace. Relearn business fundamentals in a disrupted economy.

The people who stay relevant are those who stay flexible.

Future readiness isn't about mastering every new trend.

It's about building a **mindset of adaptability** — where you're open to change, excited by learning, and fearless in reinvention.

So ask yourself:

- What am I learning today?
- What do I need to unlearn from the past?
- What should I relearn with a fresh lens?

Your degree gives you a start.
But your mindset — to evolve, adapt, and grow — will carry you through the decades ahead.

The future won't wait. But it will reward those who prepare.

So stay sharp. Stay humble. Stay hungry.

Future-ready, future-strong.

Always learning with you,
Ashish

CHAPTER XXVI

Stay Hungry for New Trends, Not Just Old Textbooks

Dear MBA Student,

Textbooks are important.
They teach you frameworks, fundamentals, and timeless theories.
But here's the truth:

The business world isn't run by what's written in old books — it's driven by emerging trends.

Markets evolve. Consumers shift. Technology disrupts.
If you want to lead in tomorrow's world, you must do more than just study the past — you need to anticipate the future.

Yes, understand Porter's Five Forces. Yes, analyze balance sheets.
But also understand:

- The rise of AI in decision-making
- The shift from shareholder to stakeholder capitalism
- The power of personal branding in the digital era
- The influence of Gen Z behavior on consumer trends
- The growth of sustainable and ethical business models

Because the professionals who spot trends early are the

ones who create impact, drive innovation, and build the future.

Here's how to stay trend-aware:

1. Follow Industry News Daily

Spend 15 minutes a day on platforms like Harvard Business Review, McKinsey Insights, Economic Times, TechCrunch, or YourStory.
Make it a habit.

2. Subscribe to Thought Leaders

Follow CEOs, entrepreneurs, marketers, and strategists on LinkedIn, YouTube, or podcasts. Their insights are real-time and often far more current than classroom content.

3. Attend Webinars, Events, and Conferences

Your learning doesn't end in the classroom. Attend guest lectures, startup expos, or online summits. That's where the future is being discussed — live.

4. Build Curiosity, Not Just Compliance

Don't read only what's assigned. Explore topics that excite you. Ask, "What's next in my industry?" Develop the habit of intellectual curiosity.

5. Apply Trends to What You Learn

Use trending topics in your case studies, presentations, and assignments. It shows you're not just a student — you're a future-ready thinker.

The best MBA students don't just study what was. They prepare for what will be.

The market rewards those who can combine strong fundamentals with fresh awareness.
So don't wait for someone to spoon-feed you the future.
Go find it. Read about it. Talk about it. Think deeply about it.

And always stay one step ahead.

Because in the real world, awareness is a superpower.

Stay curious, stay sharp,
Ashish

CHAPTER XXVII

Learn to Handle Pressure & Rejections Gracefully

Dear MBA Student,

Your MBA journey will be filled with ambition, deadlines, competition, and expectations — from yourself, your peers, your faculty, and even your family.

It's exciting.
It's intense.
And at times, it can feel overwhelming.

Not every group project will go smoothly.
Not every application will turn into an offer.
Not every effort will be appreciated.

And in those moments, you'll feel pressure. You may even face rejection.

But here's a truth that will carry you through:

Pressure doesn't break you. It reveals you.
Rejection doesn't define you. It refines you.

Pressure is a Part of the Process

Feeling anxious before a presentation, stretched during exams, or stressed during placement season? You're not

alone.
Everyone feels it — the difference lies in how you respond to it.

Here's how to deal with pressure like a pro:

- Break tasks into small, manageable actions
- Prioritize what matters instead of trying to do it all
- Breathe deeply, think clearly, and act calmly
- Ask for help — it's a strength, not a weakness

Pressure is not the enemy. Panic is. Train yourself to stay grounded.

Rejection is Not a Personal Attack

Didn't get selected in that company?
Didn't make it to the final round?
Didn't get the recognition you hoped for?

It hurts. But it doesn't mean you're not good enough.
It means something else is meant for you — or that you need to grow a bit more to be ready.

Use rejection as redirection. Ask:

- What can I learn from this?
- What do I need to improve?
- What will I do differently next time?

Remember: some of the world's best success stories started

with a no.

Grace Under Fire is a Leadership Trait

Your true character shows not when everything goes your way, but when nothing does.

Stay composed. Stay humble. Stay focused.
When you learn to smile through setbacks and rise after falls — you earn a kind of inner strength that no degree can teach.

Pressure will polish you. Rejections will shape you. Your response to both will define you.

So the next time it gets too much, don't run from it. Stand tall.
Take a break if needed. Reflect. Reset. But don't give up.

You've come this far. You're stronger than you think.

With resilience and belief,
Ashish

CHAPTER XXVIII

Build Resilience – It's Your Real Superpower

Dear MBA Student,

In a world that glorifies intelligence, confidence, and ambition — there's one trait that quietly powers success behind the scenes:

Resilience.

It's not flashy.
It doesn't win awards.
But it's the one thing that will keep you going long after others give up.

Resilience is the ability to bounce back — from failure, pressure, rejection, burnout, criticism, and chaos.
It's what allows you to bend without breaking, to pause without quitting, and to believe without proof that better days are coming.

Why is Resilience So Important in Your MBA Journey?

Because your MBA is not just about learning business — it's about learning life.

There will be moments when:

- A presentation goes horribly wrong
- You miss out on that one company you really wanted
- Your group project becomes a group mess
- You feel like you're falling behind while others are racing ahead

And in those moments, your technical skills won't save you. Your resilience will.

Here's How You Build It:

1. Normalize Struggles

Don't see setbacks as signs that something's wrong with you. See them as part of the process. Everyone struggles — the strong just don't quit.

2. Stay Focused on the Bigger Picture

Remind yourself why you started. Don't let one bad day make you doubt your whole journey.

3. Bounce Back Faster Each Time

You don't need to be unshakeable — you just need to get up one more time than you fall. Over time, the bounce-back becomes quicker and stronger.

4. Protect Your Mental Health

Sleep well. Eat right. Journal. Meditate. Talk to someone when needed. Resilience doesn't mean suffering in silence

— it means taking care of your energy so you can keep going.

5. Celebrate Small Wins

When things get tough, even finishing an assignment on time is a win. Track your progress. It builds belief.

The real superheroes in life aren't the ones who never fall — they're the ones who rise every single time, stronger, wiser, and calmer.

Resilience makes you unshakable in an unpredictable world.
It turns pressure into growth. Pain into wisdom. Delays into depth.

So, while you build your resume, don't forget to build your resilience.
Because that's the strength that will carry you long after the applause fades.

Fall. Learn. Rise. Repeat.

Unbreakable with you,
Ashish

CHAPTER XXIX

Think Like an Entrepreneur (Even If You're Not One)

Dear MBA Student,

Not everyone will launch a startup. Not everyone will pitch to investors or bootstrap a business.
And that's okay.

But here's what's not okay — going through your MBA without developing an **entrepreneurial mindset.**

You don't have to be an entrepreneur to think like one.

In fact, whether you join a big corporation, a startup, a government think tank, or even become a freelancer — thinking like an entrepreneur will make you more agile, valuable, and future-ready.

Because entrepreneurship is not just about starting something — it's about how you approach everything.

So, what does it mean to "think like an entrepreneur"?

1. Take Ownership

Entrepreneurs don't wait to be told what to do — they figure it out.
In a team, internship, or job, take full responsibility. Act

like it's your company. It builds trust and leadership.

2. Solve Problems, Don't Just Follow Instructions

Entrepreneurs spot gaps, ask better questions, and offer solutions.
In meetings or projects, be the person who thinks, "How can we make this better?"

3. Be Resourceful

An entrepreneur knows how to get things done — even without perfect resources.
Can't find the right person? Reach out.
Don't have a tool? Learn one.
Stuck? Try again differently. That's hustle.

4. Embrace Risk and Learn from Failure

The entrepreneurial mindset doesn't fear failure — it learns from it.
Pitch ideas. Try new things. Don't worry about being wrong — worry about staying stagnant.

5. Think in Terms of Value

Entrepreneurs always ask: "Am I creating value?"
In your assignments, your presentations, your job — focus on the impact you're creating, not just the task you're completing.

6. Innovate with Constraints

Startups are born with limited resources and high ambition.
That's the perfect training ground for creativity.
Can you find smarter, simpler, faster ways to get results?

7. Build a Bias for Action

Entrepreneurs don't overthink — they act.
Start that project. Reach out to that mentor. Launch that idea.
Start now. Perfect later.

The corporate world doesn't need more employees — it needs intrapreneurs.
People who think like founders, work like owners, and lead like innovators.

And when you bring that energy — you're not just adding value to your company.
You're shaping your own career, mindset, and legacy.

So, whether or not you start a business one day, start thinking like someone who could.

Because the entrepreneurial mindset isn't a job description —

It's a way of life.

Boldly with you,
Ashish

CHAPTER XXX

Life After MBA – It's a Marathon, Not a Sprint

Dear MBA Student,

As you approach the final leg of your MBA journey, the pressure to "figure it all out" starts to grow.

Placements. Packages. Roles. Designations.
It feels like everything rides on what happens in the next few months.

But here's a perspective I hope you'll carry for life:

Your career is not a sprint. It's a marathon.
And your MBA is just the starting block.

Yes, your first job matters. Yes, your placement can open doors.
But no — it doesn't define your destiny.

The truth is, the most successful people rarely had it all figured out right after graduation.
They explored. Failed. Switched. Pivoted. Learned. Grew.

So what should you remember as you step into life after MBA?

1. Don't Rush the Journey

You don't need to become a VP by 30.
You need to build the foundation that will sustain you for 30+ years.
Long-term growth requires patience, consistency, and self-awareness.

2. Your Learning Has Just Begun

An MBA gives you tools.
But applying those tools in the real world — with messy teams, real deadlines, and unpredictable clients — is where true mastery begins.

Stay a student, always.

3. Success Has Many Definitions

It's not just about salary or title.
It's about impact. Fulfillment. Freedom. Peace. Purpose.
Define what success means to you — and let that guide your choices.

4. Protect Your Energy, Not Just Your Time

Burnout is real. And avoidable.
Take care of your mental health, relationships, and inner peace. The world needs healthy achievers, not exhausted ones.

5. Build a Life, Not Just a Living

Chase goals. But also chase balance.

Travel. Reconnect. Serve. Create. Reflect.
The MBA is a big chapter — but it's not the whole story.

Don't let Day 0 pressure make you forget — you have decades ahead to shape your legacy.

What matters is not how fast you rise, but how strong and steady you build.

So breathe easy. Walk your path. Trust the process.

The race is long. But if you run it with clarity, courage, and consistency — it'll be worth every step.

Cheering for your lifelong journey,
Ashish

From Mba To Mbl (master Of Building Life)

Dear MBA Student,

As you turn the final page of this book, I want to leave you with a truth that lies beyond every degree, every placement, every ambition:

You didn't just come here to earn an MBA — you came here to become a Master of Building Life.

Yes, you'll walk out with knowledge. With case studies, frameworks, and business acumen.
But the real gift of this journey is the **person you become** — the way you think, lead, connect, grow, and respond to life.

Because the world doesn't just need MBAs.
It needs MBLs — **Masters of Building Life.**
People who know how to:

- Build careers with clarity
- Build relationships with empathy
- Build organizations with ethics
- Build lives with meaning
- And build a nation with vision

Your MBA has given you tools.
Now, your responsibility is to apply those tools — to create, to serve, to lead, and to live consciously.

This book was never about tips and tricks. It was about perspective.
A reminder that success is not a destination, but a daily discipline.
That leadership is not a role, but a responsibility.
And that learning never ends — it only evolves.

As you step into the world beyond campus, take these letters with you.
Revisit them when you feel lost. Reflect on them when you need direction.
And most importantly, write your own letters — to juniors, to peers, to your future self.

Because someday, someone will look up to you — not just for what you achieved, but for who you became.

You are not just an MBA graduate.
You are a Master of Building Life.

Live like it. Lead like it. Build like it.

With belief in your brilliance,
Ashish

The Mbl Manifesto (master Of Building Life)

I am not just an MBA graduate.
I am a builder of lives — starting with my own.

I choose clarity over confusion,
Discipline over distraction,
Purpose over popularity,
And growth over comfort.

I understand that success is not defined by job titles or paychecks —
It is measured by impact, character, and contribution.

I commit to:

- Leading with integrity, not just ambition
- Learning continuously — from books, people, and life itself
- Helping others rise as I rise
- Making my voice count for something bigger than myself
- Turning every failure into feedback, every challenge into a chance
- Staying curious, courageous, and compassionate

I will not wait for opportunities.
I will **create them.**
I will not just chase the future.
I will **build it.**

Because I am more than a student of business —
I am a **Master of Building Life.**

And this life,
I will build with purpose.

Signed,

Name: _______________________

Date: _______________________